RAISING CONFIDENT KIDS

Practical Strategies

for

Building Self-Belief

Resilience,

and

Emotional Strength

JUDY BARTKOWIAK

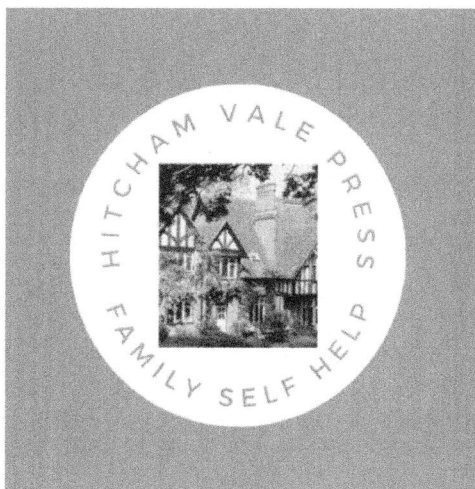

DEDICATION

Thank you for choosing this book and being willing to explore how you can make little changes that will help your child to feel more confident.

.

CONTENTS

ACKNOWLEDGMENTS

I'd like to thank everyone who reads my books and especially those who take the time to leave a review. Feedback makes a big difference to writers, especially as we spend a lot of time on our own, wondering what readers will find helpful and hoping that in some way we might make a difference in your life as a parent..

1 INTRODUCTION

Almost every mum I talk to describes their child as lacking confidence, having low self-belief, finding new situations daunting and scary, feeling anxious about tests and worrying about life in general. They lack the confidence they need to make friends and they very quickly give up and isolate themselves behind a virtual wall. It seems that children today fear failure more than anything else; be that failure socially, physically or mentally.

When I've run workshops for parents on this topic, it's clear that whilst they know they want their child to be confident, they struggle to describe what that will look, sound and feel like.

So how will they know when they have achieved it? By contrast, they can give me umpteen examples of the lack of it;

- Avoiding eye contact
- Muttering and speaking quietly or not at all when asked a question
- Reluctance to try new activities, meet new people or go to new places
- Needing to know plans ahead of time, not being comfortable with changes to them
- Disliking changes to routines and people, such as supply teachers
- Nervous about exams, tests and anything they fear they will fail at
- Asking questions when out in public or even in the classroom
- Making decisions

When asked what confidence is, their answer is that it is none of the list above but then struggled to identify what they were hoping to see when their child was not those things. In NLP (neuro linguistic programming) we call this 'away from' thinking, focusing on what we don't want.. It's actually quite complicated for the brain to be told what you don't want and have to figure out what you do want, without any clear instruction. This is why at the front end of my book I'm asking you to think about this because what you focus on, what you concentrate on, is what you get more of because your brain has been instructed to look out for it.

Another aspect to consider as we focus on confidence is the fact that children learn from you from the moment they are born and probably in utero. So how you model confidence is very important. They are observing you as you try new things, speak to people you've never met, asked questions or coped with difficult challenging situations.

I have written this book to help you guide them in raising their confidence and I have another book due out later 2025 covering resilience.

My books are based on over 20 years' coaching children and teenagers in my practice NLP & EFT Kids and before then, running focus groups as a children's Market Researcher working with toy companies.

So how else can I help you and your children?

I offer a 1:1 course for children and young people called 'Confidence and Resilience'. It comprises four one hour Zoom sessions with a workbook and a homework exercise for them to practice. It teaches children basic life skills that they may not receive at school. You can make an enquiry via my website.

I also offer training in NLP and EFT for parents or teachers who would like to learn additional skills either to work professionally with young people or to use with their family.

You can buy workbooks for early years, children, tweens, teens, new mums, teachers, work and sport on my website or of course on Amazon. This is the newest one, all about improving your sports' mindset.

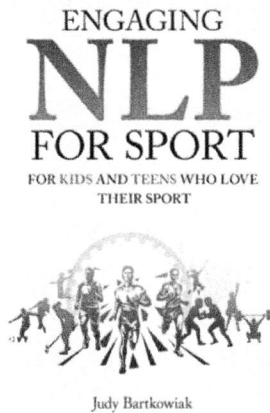

ENGAGING

NLP

FOR SPORT

FOR KIDS AND TEENS WHO LOVE
THEIR SPORT

Judy Bartkowiak

CONTACT DETAILS FOR JUDY

NLP TRAINING

NLP BOOKS

KIDS COACHING

Website judybartkowiak.com

2 HOW DO YOU RECOGNISE CONFIDENCE?

Pay attention when your child is confident. I've discovered through my years of coaching and teaching that parents tend to notice when their child is anxious and when they are not confident but don't seem to see when they are. Is that because we have to act and do something when there's a problem that needs fixing and can leave things be and assume everything is OK the rest of the time?

Children and young people may tell us about something that happened at school, perhaps they're being bullied, the teacher doesn't seem to like them much, and they don't have many friends, that sort of thing. It could manifest itself in them hiding behind you when you speak to someone or they won't put themselves forward or initiate a conversation. Perhaps they avoid eye contact and opportunities to engage. We notice these things but miss evidence that they are confident in other ways or at other times.

We tend to have our own idea of what a confident child or young person should do and say in different situations and when ours fall short we blame ourselves and worry about how their lack of confidence will get in the way of them achieving all they could achieve in life.

This is particularly so when we feel that we lack confidence ourselves and fear that this has been passed on to our children.

You will find as a parent or a teacher that where you focus, what you concentrate your attention on, is what you see more and more and what you ultimately get more of. So the more you notice your child not being confident or your own signs of lack of confidence, the more you'll actually experience it.

Some people believe that you either have confidence or you don't and that's the end of it. They believe confidence can't be taught. I disagree. You can learn to be confident yourself and you can pass these skills on to your children. This is what we will be learning in this book, how to give our children and young people the gift of confidence.

First let's just think about how you define confidence, what do you personally look for as signs of confidence in your child? When I asked some mums who liked my Facebook Page what signs of confidence they wanted to see as their children develop they said.....

"As a mum of a 14-year-old girl who has confidence and self-esteem issues I would love to see her being confident enough to chat openly with others. A friend is also here with me and she would love to see her 15-year-old nephew confident in approaching shop keepers. My daughter says she would just like to be confident!!"

"To accept themselves as they're going through adolescence.

So many teenagers and younger children become body-conscious and end up with no confidence and low self-esteem not to mention eating disorders. Their belief is that society expects them to look a certain way; you only have to look in fashion magazines etc."

"Confidence in speaking to express their feelings, confidence to do something and be proud of themselves."

"An ability to converse with adults, look them in the eye and actually have a conversation. I have noticed my 11-year-old starting to do this and I'm so proud of him. Previously he would grunt and hide in his room. Connected to this would also be an ability to initiate conversations, and to ask for things in shops, doctor's surgeries, anywhere really instead of asking me to do it for him."

"The confidence to be kind, caring and compassionate to others without the fear of being made a fool of by their peers! This confident ability would not only help them but encourage others to do the same making our world a far better place in the future if not now!"

"The signs of confidence I look for in my kids are in their beliefs - does my child generally believe him/herself to be able to learn new things and be capable of gaining a level of competence of their own choosing?"

Grab a pen and a pad or use the 'notes' function on your phone to write down what exactly <u>you</u> want to see in terms of signs of confidence. I say 'exactly' for a reason. When we are vague about what we believe confidence to be then how will we recognise it?

The best way to do this exercise is to complete the sentence:

The signs of confidence I'd like to see in my child / teenager are…………..

Be curious. Every day ask yourself

"I wonder what signs of confidence I will see today?'

What you look out for, you will see more examples of. Unfortunately that applies to things you don't want to see as well.

A dad client of mine told me that his father had told him when he was young "Son, being a father is the hardest thing you will ever do in life"

So guess what he was always focusing on with his two boys?

Guess what he was seeing?

What was he missing?

3 HOW CAN YOU SHOW THEM CONFIDENCE?

Children learn confidence from you.

Look back at the list that you've written. How do you demonstrate or 'model' those signs of confidence that you're looking for in your child? The way children learn is by watching and listening. They observe their parents in many different situations and through this they learn how to make friends, how to cope with disappointments, how to manage their anger, how to express themselves, how to learn and of course the subject of this book, how to be confident.

However, even when you are not particularly confident yourself you can still pass on confidence once you know the signs because you can show them what confidence looks, sounds and feels like.

Some of us may have had experiences in our own life as a child which resulted in our lacking confidence. Parents or teachers who put you down, a bereavement, divorce or disability that meant you felt bad about yourself; these can result in having low self-esteem.

When someone significant in the family or at school is critical or negative about you or your behaviour, children grow up questioning their ability and self-worth. But even if this <u>was</u> your experience and even if you don't have great self-confidence yourself this does not mean that this can't change. Nor does it mean that your children will lack confidence. You can learn to be confident and pass this on to your children and everyone you come into contact with. It will change your life in so many ways. Think about it now.

What messages did you get from your parents about who you were? …………………..

What about in school? Were your teachers encouraging and positive about your contributions in class and your work?

Did you excel in sport and get your self-confidence from that?

Were you creative and complimented for your makes?

When we take our confidence from other people, this is called '*external referencing*' and when we check in with ourselves and take our confidence from within, that is '*internal referencing*'. You don't have control over other people so you will be more confident when you internally reference.

When I am confident I will be able to…………

When my child/teenager is confident they will be able to…………..

4 WHY DO WE NEED CONFIDENCE?

Confident people look, sound and feel different to be around. We listen when they say something, we do what they ask, we look at them and notice their presence.

We know that our children need confidence in life in order to stand up for themselves and express their needs and opinions. As it becomes harder to get a job, we know that our children are going to have to rely on more than just an education. They will need to mix socially and network in order to get ahead. One day they will meet someone they love, settle down and have a family of their own and we want them to have the confidence to make the right decisions and develop healthy and equal relationships based on trust and respect. Self-esteem is essential for healthy development of the mind and body.

We need confidence as parents to discipline our children, guide their decision-making and lead them by good example. We need confidence in the workplace to keep our job, run our business successfully and develop our career. In our social life confidence enables us to build rapport with new people we meet, maintain friendships and discover new hobbies and interests, learn new skills and show our children that life is more than just work.

What's more, being able to say 'no' and staying true to your beliefs and values rather than being drawn along by peers will keep you and your child safe and happy.

I know that nowadays we are encouraged to find ways to say "yes" whilst actually meaning "no" in other words creating a positive outcome for your child although not agreeing to what is requested. This can sometimes be quite a challenge, can't it? It's something I struggle with as a granny having brought my children up to understand that 'no is no'! But things change and now I need to adapt but I do wonder how children then learn to say 'no' themselves when they are being asked to do something they don't want to do such as taking drugs, alcohol or sex. My feeling is that there should still be a 'no' reserved for more serious or urgent situations such as if a child is about to put their hand on a hotplate or knock something off a table.

Boundaries, being able to communicate and maintain the house or family rules are a sign of confident leadership and can give children and teens a sense of security. When boundaries are inconsistent, there can be a feeling of uncertainty as to what is right and what is wrong and this can be confusing and unsettling.

I need my child to be confident so that they……………

I need to a confident parent so that I ………………………

5. HOW TO LOOK CONFIDENT

It is well known that we make important and long-lasting assumptions about people in the first few seconds of seeing them, before we've even spoken. We look at a person's demeanor, how they hold themselves generally. We notice what they're wearing, style, colours, condition, whether it fits them and suits them. We note how they're standing or sitting, where they're looking, their facial expression, their eyes, hair, hand movements and so the list goes on.

Think about how you look right now. If someone were to meet you at this moment would they think you were confident? What could you do to alter their opinion? How could you give the impression of confidence simply by changing how you look, stand or hold yourself generally? Note them down.

When I do these things I look more confident............

There are several tips I can pass on to you and I'd like you to have a go at these now.

1. **Stand upright** with both your legs firmly planted on the floor slightly apart and arms still. Make sure your shoulders are relaxed and your head nicely positioned in the middle. Like this you look aligned. When you are positioned in this way you also feel more aligned and in tune with yourself. When we take on a certain physiology to look as if we are aligned and in control, because our mind and our body are connected, we also get the feeling of being aligned.

2. You can have a go at the seated version of this because this is useful in the classroom and at work.

3. Give good **eye contact**. Look people in the eye, not of course with a glare but in a relaxed way so that you don't threaten them but meet their look rather than looking away. When you look away or look down you do not look confident and instead you look vulnerable. In such a vulnerable physiology you are more likely to be criticized, picked on and bullied by those who seek out weaker people as prey. Too much eye contact or when it is intense can give the opposite impression but can also be used effectively. For example, as a parent you might want to experiment with using eye contact to communicate with your child. Avoid eye contact when they are misbehaving, give good eye contact when all's well and when you want to communicate displeasure, give intense eye contact.

4. **Be still**. Fidgeting and busy hand movements distract from what you are saying or doing and give the impression of being unsure. You can use your hands but do it deliberately to illustrate a point rather than flapping away, especially in front of your face. Touching your hair and face also indicates lack of confidence. Young people tend to do this quite a bit but it doesn't have a place in a situation where they want to appear confident.

5. **Choice of clothes**. Like it or not, you are assumed to have made a conscious decision to wear what you have chosen to wear. What you are wearing tells other people something about you, as does your choice of how much make up to wear. Choose clothes that fit; gaping tops, stomach bulging over trouser tops and so on simply indicate that you are not buying the right size clothes. Clothes need to be fashionable but not suitable for the night club and the colours should co-ordinate and suit your skin tone and colouring. Decide consciously what look you want for the occasion because it is your choice what you communicate to others about yourself so take control of it.

6. **Move slowly**. Running about and fidgeting does not inspire confidence. You look out of control. Make your movements deliberate and fluid so that you look as if you know what you're doing and where you're going.

7. **Smile**. There may be situations where smiling isn't appropriate but in most situations a smile will improve rapport and create the impression that you are confident and have self-worth. Your smile will give the person you are with a sense of self-worth as well, so it's mutually beneficial.

Which of these resonates most with you?

Are you someone who rushes about?

Do you use your hands a lot?

Do you just put on the first thing to hand in the morning?

All of these things are signs of lack of confidence. You will communicate confidence and control when you practice these non-verbal cues.

Why would you want to?

Because when you communicate confidence to your children and teenagers they get it. Yes, they learn from you. They learn by example. You can tell them until you get hoarse, you can give them books and articles to read but when you demonstrate what you want them to learn from you, they totally get it.

The other reason for using these non-verbal cues is to manage your state. Your state is your mood or state of mind. When we want to be calm, communicate control and manage difficult situations we can do this in a more resourceful way if we appear to be aligned and in control of our body. Imagine telling off your child from another room with no eye contact as you're rushing about looking for a stray school shoe?! Yes I know, we all do it but just how effective is it?

Think for a moment about the people you know who you would describe as confident and self-assured? Put a face to the name and a body. Now close your eyes and visualise them. Imagine them there in front of you. How do they move and how do they hold themselves.

How many of these 'boxes' do they tick?

Stand / sit still

Good eye contact

Be still

Good choice of clothes

Move slowly

Smile

In future when I want to show that I am confident I will……

So there are many non-verbal signs of confidence we can use to create the illusion of confidence for those times when we need it.

Do you have clothes you wear when you want to feel confident?

Maybe jewellery or accessories, scarves, handbag?

You'll find that when we act 'as if' we are confident, because our mind and body are connected, we feel confident inside as well.

This can be enhanced by becoming aware of our values. On what do we place value? What is important to us? What do we believe in and are we living our life according to those beliefs? When we are aligned spiritually and mentally this translates into our body so that it too is aligned. Encourage children as they grow up to live according to their beliefs and values. When they are young these will probably be the same as yours but as they learn more about the world, meet new people, travel and read, they will develop their own values and beliefs.

Try this affirmation and remember that we word affirmations in the present tense even though these are what we want for the future.

" I am confident"

"I am a confident parent"

6 HOW TO SOUND CONFIDENT

Although we make our first judgement based on non-verbal cues, as soon as someone speaks, the **verbal** cues take over. Firstly let's ignore content for the moment and just focus on tone of voice because again we notice this more than the content of what is said.

1. **Speak slowly**. Just as moving about and flapping your arms about while you're speaking distracts the listener from paying attention to your voice, speaking fast makes you difficult to follow. Lots of highly visual creative people speak fast as they mentally translate the images in their head into speech but unless their listener is also visual, it will be a struggle for someone to understand the concepts they are describing. Also, be aware that nowadays we live in a multi-cultural society where for many, English isn't their first language.

2. Speak **loud** enough so that the other person can hear. This seems rather obvious but as soon as someone has

to struggle to listen to you, they won't bother unless they have to. When people lack confidence they are inclined to mutter and mumble and in some group exercises their input will be missed.

3. **Pitch** your voice midway between high and low for good communication and the impression that what you have to say is important and worth listening to. High pitch sounds hysterical and out of control. Low pitch sounds a bit sinister. Practice by using the voice recorder on your phone.

4. **Breathe**. It can be exhausting listening to someone speaking with no pauses between sentences and as if they're in a race. Break up sentences and breathe so that you give the impression that you know what you want to say and that it is important. If there are no gaps for the other person to engage in the conversation, they soon lose interest.

5. **Initiate conversation.** Children need to be able to walk up to someone and start a conversation so ask them to think of a few topics or comments that they can have ready for this. Show them how you do it.

6. **Ask questions**. Engage the other person in your conversation either by asking them a specific question or by adding a 'yes tag' such as 'don't you?' or 'wouldn't you?' which invites agreement. In this way you show that their opinion is of interest and that you are confident enough to include them in the conversation.

Ask your child or young person to think about someone whom they consider to be confident. How does this person demonstrate these qualities? Can they add any other things they do which gives them the impression that they have high self-esteem? When children 'channel' this confident friend of theirs, they can imagine how they would behave in different situations and copy them. What belief has their confident friend got that enables them to be confident? Can they borrow that belief?

The person I'm thinking of who seems really confident is..............

7 HOW TO SPEAK WITH CONFIDENCE

So now let's move on to the **content**. What you actually say does matter of course even though the aforementioned non-verbal cues are the first to be noticed. There are three areas which need to be avoided when you want to be confident and appear to be confident.

Generalisations

When you declare that 'everybody' or 'no-one' says or does something this is very unlikely to be the case and it lowers your credibility; not just of what you're saying at the time but of everything else you say. Similarly words like 'always' and 'never' aren't likely to be true. When we generalise, it invites others to question what we are saying which isn't a very confident place to be.

When attempting to persuade your teenager to revise for example, telling them that 'everyone knows you have to revise' or that 'no-one else will leave it until the day before' will not hold sway because they will surely tell you of exceptions.

You miss out on important learning when you generalise because it will be the one time when something worked, when you felt confident, when you felt great, that gives you the successful strategy. By focusing on all the other times when things didn't go so well just reinforces the losing strategy.

Distortions

This is when we pass on our responsibility for our own emotions by saying things like 'you make me really cross' or 'you've made me very upset'. Our emotions are our own choice, however tempting it might be to blame someone else. When we do this we lose confidence by showing that we can't take this responsibility on board and need to offload it onto others.

When your child says that someone made them do something, say something or behave in a certain way, ask "how did they do that exactly, how did they make you do that?" Invite them to consider what other choices they had. Choices give them flexibility and flexibility gives them control. Control of the situation is what we seek in self-esteem.

Mind—reading is another form of distortion. Avoid assuming you know what someone else is thinking e.g. "I know you'll disagree but..............". This is not a confident start to any conversation and puts yourself in a position where rapport will be hard to achieve. You have already mismatched and indicated that this is your preferred way of conversing. Another form of mind-reading is predicting the future e.g. "You'll end up on benefits if you don't work hard at school." Even if you're sure you're right, it is not possible to predict this. It does not look confident to say things that you can't know for sure so it's better to own up and phrase it simply as your own opinion or fear.

Deletions

We frequently delete information that our listener needs in order to make sense of what we're saying. When someone doesn't understand us and we miscommunicate in some way we get a sense of low self-esteem, yet by ensuring all the information is there we can overcome this and communicate in confidence. An example of this would be 'that was so much better'. We have not explained what 'that' was and how it was better, better than what? I've heard teenagers say "I wish I was more confident." I need to know more. I ask "in what way confident?", "when?" "where", "with whom?". There's lots of essential missing information.

Listen to how confident people talk. They express themselves clearly and you understand what they are saying.

Initiating conversation

You may notice that confident people often initiate conversation. They may go up to a stranger and start chatting. As children get older their confidence grows and they begin to take some risks in this area. However, we can get them used to this process if we encourage them while young to ask for things rather than anticipating help.

After all, we know our children and can guess what they want without having to ask, but if you gradually start to expect confident communication from your toddler they will be quite used to asking for things by the time they are at school.

For example, get them to ask where the toilet is in the doctor's surgery or at the dentist or ask where things are in the supermarket Make sure they associate this with confidence by giving them specific feedback such as "Well done that was a sign of how confident you're getting now."

Expressing opinions

Being confident isn't just about being able to converse with people; it's also about expressing yourself and being true to your values and beliefs. This is also true for children and much more so for teenagers who have a well-developed sense of their own identity which may be different from their parents and their peers. Being able to be themselves and not conform to society stereotypes in terms of fashion, body shape, celebrity culture and so on, all contribute to them becoming 'their own person' and this is a sign of confidence. When your child expresses an opinion that seems to have been thought through and is true to their values, notice it and mark it out as a sign of confidence. It can be tempting when the opinion differs from yours to argue or find it annoying that they are expressing a different opinion but remember it is their opinion. It may change but for the moment this is their belief.

I believe that confidence is about being comfortable in one's own skin. In France they say 'bien dans sa peau' which means the same thing. This is not necessarily about what people say or what they do but is more of a feeling one gets in their company. It is about feeling aligned and at one with the world. This is not usually a constant state but it's good to recognise it when you have it so you recognise it next time. This is a gift to pass on to your children. When they seem comfortable in their own skin, check it out and make them aware of it so it becomes a desirable state for them in the future.

I have shared with you a number of ways for you to recognise confidence in yourself, others and in your children. I have also explained how to look and sound confident and how to speak confidently. Note what you've learnt before moving on to the next section. Remember you are their model for confidence so when you use these signs of confidence yourself, they will follow your lead.

These are the changes I can make in order to be confident and model it for my children………………

8 CONFIDENCE BOOSTERS

We all have days when we wish we felt more inspired, full of energy and could find the right words for the occasion. On days like that everyone else seems to be cleverer, more attractive, funnier or have whatever we feel we are lacking. Their children seem better behaved, socially competent, brighter and so on. These are days when we need to raise our self-esteem. When we can raise our own, we are then in a great place to show our children how to raise theirs. So how do we do it?

On the following pages you will find a number of tips for boosting your child's confidence (and your own of course!). Experiment, your child will respond better to some than others and the ground will shift all the time so what works today won't work next week so do something else!

1. __CONTROL YOUR STATE__

You know about how to recognise confidence in others through the non-verbal cues of confidence. We can use this device, this mind/body connection to change our state deliberately when we need to. Say, for example, your child is feeling overwhelmed by a situation, out of control and feels low in confidence. STOP. Tell them to take control of their state and change it. Go through the tips I've mentioned by telling them to

Stand or sit still

Be still

Move slowly

Give you eye contact

There's not much you can do about clothes at a moment's notice but you can certainly slow everything down and get them to give you eye contact.

Another way to control your state is to anchor a resourceful state. Have you heard of Pavlov's dogs? Pavlov rang a bell when he fed his dogs and after a while they began to expect food whenever they heard the bell. Then he stopped feeding them (not for long I hope!) and just rang the bell. They responded in just the same way as they did just before he fed them; they salivated and got excited. They had learned to associate the bell with food. Imagine if we could develop some sort of action or sound that would associate us with confidence. Well this is what anchoring is. This is how we do it.

Step 1. Ask your child to make a 'thumbs up' sign. This will be the anchor equivalent to the bell ringing sound.

Step 2. Ask them to think about a time when they felt really super confident and when they are totally in the zone tell them to use the 'thumbs up' sign.

Step 3. Break state. This means that they shake themselves in between each anchoring.

Step 4. Repeat, thinking of other times when they have felt confident. Remember to use the anchor each time.

Step 5. Tell them to think about something coming up that they were feeling a bit anxious about but this time use the anchor to encourage them to think about how well it will go.

You can suggest any anchor you want. The thumbs up is quite a universal one but you can also suggest an OK sign or they could think of a place that's special to them, a song they like or a different action. They can anchor different states, not just confidence. They can anchor feeling brave (for the dentist or injections), feeling calm (for exams), feeling energised (for a race) and so on. They will need to use a different anchor for each one though so that each state has its own anchor.

Children who suffer from anger or behavioural issues often benefit from having an anchor to remind them and associate into a more resourceful state.

When your children and teenagers are going to be in a stressful situation when it might be important to convey an illusion of being confident and in control, tell them to take control of their body first.

Sit or stand in alignment, with their head straight, keeping arms and legs still and use minimal movement. Then they can ground themselves by imagining they are a tree putting down roots deep into the ground. They can wave their branches and bend in the wind but their feet should stay firmly planted on the ground, connecting with the earth below and the sky above.

2. __LOOK UP__

Another great tip is to tell them to look up. When we look down we move into our feelings and dwell on those negative feelings about ourselves and how lacking in confidence we feel. As we look up we can imagine possibilities, more positive thoughts and feelings. Just try it with your child or teenager. When they next seem to lack confidence ask them to look up and imagine things going well.

3. GIVE HELPFUL FEEDBACK

We each have a preference for whether we notice what we see (visual), what we hear (auditory) or what we feel and do (kinaesthetic).

Knowing which your child prefers will help you to know what to say to boost their confidence. For example, a visual child will respond best to a comment using visual words such as "Look how well you're working today on your math's homework."

An auditory child will respond best to words he recognises such as "Aunt May was interested to hear about your History project, she told me you explained it very well."

A kinaesthetic child is listening for action words. "You grasped the plot of that TV programme very quickly; I was struggling to follow it."

Think about your own child which do you think they prefer?

Are they more visual, auditory or kinaesthetic?

How could you adapt your praise to suit their preference so you communicate in their language?

Make a note of a few words to use next time.

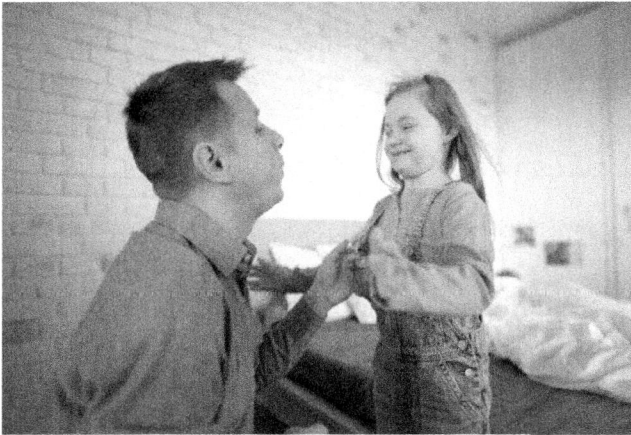

As a parent I'm sure you know when they need a confidence boost and know what to say but does it always work? Possibly not. The reason for this is because they know you love them and will probably say anything that you think will help. They do not trust you to be discerning. You will say what you think they want to hear and they'll hear it but it may not make the difference that will change how they feel right now.

Even children who lack confidence quite often will still occasionally demonstrate it but what they need is the skill to access that confidence at any time. First they need to recognise it. The last section gave you all the cues you need to recognise it yourself so you can spot it in them and point it out so they recognise it too.

Be Specific

Remember when you spot it, be specific. Say exactly what you noticed that was a sign of confidence. That way they know what the structure is. It gives them a label to apply to their behaviour e.g. 'so that behaviour is called confidence and I have it'. You can do this at a very young age.

Mark it out

Children sometimes need some illumination when it comes to confidence. So when you notice your child being confident by asking for something, give them specific feedback about what they've done so they can integrate it in the right filing cabinet in their brain as 'confidence'. Say "that was confident of you Jack".

Generalisations

I have introduced you to deletions, distortions and generalisations and advising you to avoid them when you want to show confidence. When we have no self-esteem we tend to generalise saying for example, that we 'never' know what to say or that 'everyone's' children are better behaved, we 'always' get tongue tied and have 'no' friends. When you hear these types of generalisations from your child look for the exceptions: "Well the other day I noticed you were chatting to Phoebe as you walked out of school". We don't help when we disagree with them or when we just praise in a random sort of way but when we are specific, give an example and stick to what we've actually observed rather than expressing our own personal opinion such as "Well I think you are."

Deletions

Similarly when they use a deletion by being extremely vague you can respond by asking them for more detail. For example when a child says "I'm no good at sport." This is very vague and therefore probably not true. Ask them "which sports do you think you <u>are</u> good at?" which prompts them to think positively about those they are better at.

Distortions

When children distort information in a way that lowers their self-esteem by saying that someone 'made' them feel stupid or 'didn't let' them say anything we can challenge them by asking "how did they do that?" because no-one can really make us feel something, our feelings are our own choice. Another form of distortion is 'mind reading' when our child says "they think I am…….". He has absolutely no way of knowing what they are thinking. He is guessing. They may say that he is ……but that doesn't mean they think it. They are saying something to get a reaction and it's working. We need to teach our child a different response to give them choices.

Flexibility

The person with the most flexibility has the most control in any situation so by giving our child choices we are giving him more control. How we respond to something is our choice so our children at an early age (the sooner the better) need to learn that their behaviour is their own choice. This is a way to boost their confidence as it puts the ball in their court. They can choose how to respond, what to say and do and by taking responsibility they gain self-respect and self-worth. This leads to feelings of confidence as they get older. You can start this when they are just toddlers as they drop something instead of you simply picking it up, you could ask them, "what do you think we need to do now........well done.

Yes tag

It's good to take responsibility for our accidents, isn't it?" Note the use of the 'yes tag' "isn't it?" which prompts an answer in the affirmative i.e. "yes". We use this slightly hypnotic language when we want our children and teenagers to engage and respond to our suggestion.

Think about the things your child says and consider how you could respond differently so that they start to take responsibility for how they react and start building their confidence

In recent years parents have been advised by the experts to encourage good behaviour by praising their children. This is a very good idea and does work well in raising confidence. However, children need the feedback to be specific so they can learn from it. Here are some tips about giving your child effective or resourceful feedback.

1. Give it at the time, immediately so they know what behaviour you're referring to. As children get to their teens the time lag can be longer.

2. Give it with eye contact.

3. Think about your positive intention which is what they will get learning from it so express it with that in mind. This is about them, not about you.

4. Mention the specific thing that they did or said that you noticed.

5. Link it to what that means at a bigger chunk or concept level so "I noticed that you came over to help me with the dishes even though I know you were busy doing your homework. That shows you put someone else's needs before your own. That was kind of you."

Children need to know how to file away feedback and by linking it in this way you have given them information about their identity. They know that this behaviour is kind and that if they want to be kind this is the sort of thing to do, to put someone else's needs before their own. It is much more useful to provide this detail. A simple 'thank you' or 'that was kind' does not give them enough information.

Next time they want to be kind they know how to do it and they know it is something that is appreciated and makes them feel good. It gives them self-esteem.

Give your feedback from the heart with a positive intention in your mind.

4. <u>COMMUNICATE IN THEIR LANGUAGE</u>

As well as children having a preference for visual, auditory or kinaesthetic they have what we call in NLP (neuro linguistic programming) meta-programmes which define how they process their world. They are

Concept / Detail

Choices / Process

Towards /Away from

Internal / External

Match / Mismatch

Concept / Detail

Some children like to work in concepts with big general ideas and others like the detail and small bite size pieces of information. If your child likes detail for example, they can feel overwhelmed and out of depth and lack confidence in situations where they have to come up with ideas. They would of course have far more confidence though working through the detail of someone else's idea. Similarly those who like concepts will lack confidence when they have to work with detail. Hence children will lack confidence in some subjects and excel in others. No one way is better and ideally teams at work are made up of both types. If your child lacks confidence in one area, notice where their strengths lie and point them out.

Which does your child prefer?

Choices / Process

Some children like to have options or choices so they can decide what they want but others find choices irritating and just want to go through a process from A-Z. Again, one is not better than another. A child who wants choices will be thrown by a process instruction such as 'do this, then that...' and a process child will be confused when give choices. Their reactions may seem like lack of confidence but may in fact simply reflect a different way their brain works. If your child gets flustered in a choice situation, don't give them one. If they respond badly to being given no choice then give them choice but only options that you choose.

Which does your child prefer?

Towards/ Away from

We tend to have either a 'towards' orientation or 'away from'. 'Towards' is when we have goals and things we actively want to do. 'Away from' is when we want to avoid something. For example, let's say our child is slow getting dressed and we need to leave for school or work. They may be slow because they want to carry on playing (towards – something they want to do more than going to school) or because they don't want to go to school (away from).

A 'towards' child will respond best to talking about what will be fun at school that day, something they will enjoy or a friend they like playing with because those are all 'towards'.

An 'away from' child needs reminding that if they don't hurry up they will get into trouble at school for being late (away from) and their friends will be cross because they aren't there to play with them, and so on. The implication for confidence is this:

A 'towards' child may not be avoiding situations in which they don't feel confident, they are choosing a more appealing option which could be about getting attention from you, a cuddle, reassurance, a helping hand.

An 'away from' child when they lack confidence is more about avoiding situations that are stressful or awkward so you need to remind them of what else they will avoid by taking the more confident route. You could say "If you do this now the teacher won't get cross with you" (you need an 'away from' sentiment) or "If you tell me who broke the mug I won't get cross" ('away from' again).

Which does your child prefer?

Internal / External

Internal and external reference is about where we place our focus. When we look to others for reassurance that we're on the right track we are 'externally referenced' and when we rely on our own instincts we are 'internally referenced'. As you can imagine, someone who looks to others for affirmation is likely to lack confidence in situations where it isn't forthcoming.

If you are forever praising your child you are effectively conditioning him or her to look for approval from others, which is a rather uncertain situation because one cannot control the environment outside the home. This can lead to a child starting school and unless the teacher is constantly complimenting them they will feel they're not doing well and will lack confidence. We can avoid this by encouraging our children when they are still young and spending more time with us, to start internal referencing from a young age. We can ask them, "I thought you did that really well, but what did you think?" By placing the question to them after the word 'but' we emphasise that part of the sentence. Everything before the 'but' is played down. Children focus on what comes after the 'but'.

We don't want children to be totally internally referenced of course because they wouldn't care what other people think. Ideally, we want them to be able to choose where on the continuum they need to be in specific situation. Encourage them to check in with their own values and beliefs i.e. "I know they think this, but what do I think?"

Which does your child prefer?

Match/ Mismatch

We match when we agree with someone or do something similar and mismatching is the opposite. It is much easier to get on with people when we match. We come across as more confident too when we match so encourage your child to match others. When they disagree with someone they can do this in rapport by saying something like "that's interesting and I'm wondering………."

When your child mismatches you by disagreeing as teenagers need to do at some point in order to break the umbilical cord and stretch their wings, encourage them to express themselves by being curious and asking them more about what they're saying. Be curious. Their map is different from ours.

Which does your child prefer?

5. <u>OVERCOME THEIR LIMITING BELIEFS</u>

The "I can't………"

In NLP we call this a 'limiting belief' and what it means is that your child has consciously decided that they don't have the skill to do something. How tempting it is as a loving parent to say "You can!" because we believe in our children and know that they do have the skill to do that thing. However, this really is not a helpful response. Better instead to acknowledge and accept that at this moment this is their belief. Beliefs change. Just as once they believed in Father Christmas or the Tooth Fairy; they now know that it is you or your partner. Their belief has changed based on information. Maybe they saw you one night popping the money under the pillow or someone told them at school or perhaps one of the presents in their sack was something they'd seen you buy! Either way, beliefs change. Your beliefs have changed. Your beliefs about parenting have changed and are constantly changing as your children get older so why wouldn't their beliefs change?

So accept this belief and realise that if you want them to change their belief they need evidence, knowledge, and new awareness. You need to start thinking about the skill they need to be able to do it. You could ask them too, "What do you need to be able to do that?" and you can also invite them to think about how much they want to do it by asking "what if you could do it, how would that feel? What else might you be able to do?" Unless children have an investment in doing something, unless they want the result, they won't do it.

Do NOT use the word TRY. This is an unhelpful word and gives your child an excuse on a plate. When you say "Try and do it" that means "have a go but I don't think you'll succeed." "Just try and do it" means "I know you won't succeed but if you want to give it your best shot then go ahead but if I were you I wouldn't bother."

There's a huge difference between "Do it" and "Try to do it." Tell your child to 'do it' and they know you mean business and you believe they can do it. If they don't succeed they are disobeying you which to them will carry more serious consequences than if they try but don't' succeed in which case they can say "well I tried."

Drill down with the skills needed for the task so you have a bite-size skill. By this I mean 'needing to be good at maths' is big chunk but 'knowing your 6 times tables' is small chunk and knowing 'what 6 x 7 makes' is even smaller. Check out whether your child agrees they have the skill they need and once this is in place, leave them to get on with it so they can get the sense of self-worth by completing the task on their own.

What will make the difference to the result is how well you define the skill needed and how creative and curious you can be about where they have that skill or something like it.

Your child will gain confidence through this process because they will realise they have lots of skills that they can transfer to other areas of their life.

But what is a skill? A skill is anything they can do well. It even includes things you don't like them doing. For example a child who can lie well must have skills to understand how to lie well; acting skills, knowing you well enough to convince you, caring about you enough not to trouble you with the truth and so on. A younger child having a tantrum (or a teenager having one!) has the skills of being able to express themselves and not bottling it up (even if you'd prefer it if they did) making their voice carry, not minding what you or anyone around thinks of them. They probably have the skills to be an actor, to present well, to lead people in difficult decisions.

You love your child and can think where you've seen evidence of the skill they need so you can remind them of it. This will boost their confidence especially if they agree that they do have the skill you've mentioned. When they manage to complete the task they were attempting they will have even more confidence.

6. <u>SPEAK TO THEM IN ADULT MODE</u>

Have you heard of **Transactional Analysis**? Eric Berne talks about everyone having an 'adult', 'parent' and 'child' in their heads. He calls them 'ego states'.

The '*controlling parent*' is the side of us that says we '*must*' or '*should*' do something. It is the way parents usually talk to children which is fine but when we talk to our colleagues like this it isn't appropriate or helpful. The 'nurturing parent' in you wants to protect and nurture.

The '*rebellious child'* is the part of us that throws a tantrum and gets angry and the '*loving child*' needs love and affection, cries and laughs. This is how children usually feel, they express what they feel when they feel it and want to be cared for. This is an appropriate way for a child to behave but again this won't work very well when talking to your work colleagues or clients!

The '*adult*' reasons, observes and is logical. It is the way we communicate most of the time as an adult and it is the most resourceful way to communicate.

One wouldn't want to use just one of these options available to us but we have access to each one at different times when the need arises. Even small children have all of these options and know what they 'should do' (parent), 'could do' (adult) and 'want to do' (child).

Here is an example:

Child (in adult mode asking for information) "Where are my school shoes?"

Parent (in child mode expressing annoyance) "Where you left them. This happens every morning. It makes me so cross."

Notice which mode your child is using at different times. They will be more confident in 'adult' mode where they have access to their skills and reasoning ability. Adult mode is what's needed to make decisions. It is the part of you that weighs up the options and foresees what could happen, requests information and processes it to encourage children to make decisions from a very early age. Some parents offer their children choices about what to eat but this isn't a great idea as their decision may not be what you had in mind. Offer them a decision within what you have decided so a choice between two healthy options or a choice of where to go first when you have two places you need to visit.

This is of course also true for you! Instead of constantly being in parent mode telling children what they 'should' do or telling yourself what you 'ought to do', allow yourself and them permission to do what you or they 'could do'. We all need some fun so sometimes do what you 'want' to do. There needs to be a balance otherwise meals wouldn't get cooked, jobs done, homework done; but teach children to recognise these three states so they have choices. Choices enhance confidence.

7. GIVE THEM RESPONSIBILITY

Your children will be more confident when they take responsibility for themselves and don't expect others to do so by blaming them or the weather, the bus being late and so on. When we blame others and don't take responsibility we are being 'at effect' and when we take the responsibility we are 'at cause'.

Another rule of three is the **Drama Triangle**. There are three states again; victim, persecutor and rescuer. The 'victim' is the 'poor me' in the situation; the person who feels put upon, blamed, inadequate. Children and teenagers become victims when they feel they are persecuted in some way. They are rescued by someone, maybe mum or a teacher, who helps them and for a while that's fine. They may resort to food, drugs, cigarettes and alcohol to rescue them so temporarily they feel better.

Eventually though the rescuer gets fed up with rescuing and not being appreciated and becomes a persecutor getting cross with the victim. The roles move around the triangle as no-one takes any responsibility for the situation by stepping out of the triangle.

When parents over-protect and 'helicopter parent' they are being rescuers. This denies the child the opportunity to take responsibility for themselves, their safety, decisions, choice of friends and so on. Whilst the rescuer means well and their intentions are positive, the result is that the child remains dependent and over time this leads to resentment of the rescuer. They need to know that it's OK to fail and sometimes we do feel sad, or angry. It's part of life's lessons to learn to overcome disappointments.

Ultimately children will have more confidence when they are allowed to take responsibility for themselves, make a few mistakes but learn from them. By doing everything for our children we are denying them the opportunity to gain confidence from learning to do things for themselves.

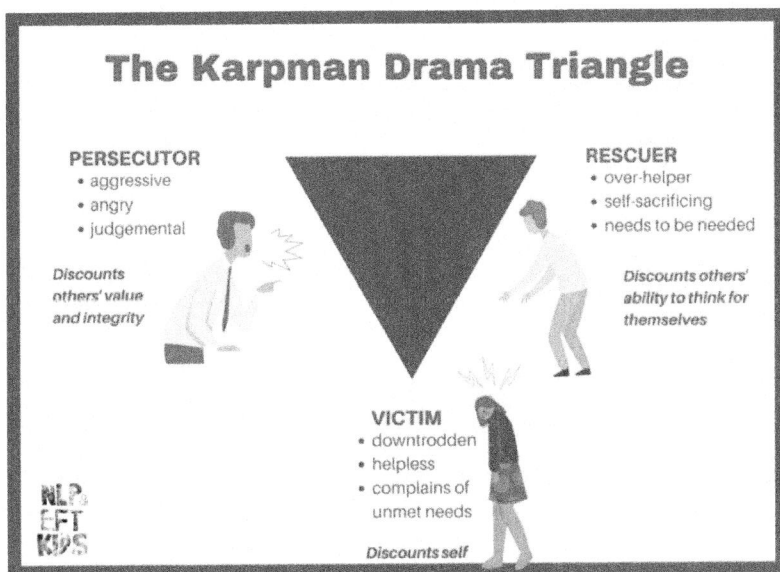

The Karpman Drama Triangle

PERSECUTOR
• aggressive
• angry
• judgemental

Discounts others' value and integrity

RESCUER
• over-helper
• self-sacrificing
• needs to be needed

Discounts others' ability to think for themselves

VICTIM
• downtrodden
• helpless
• complains of unmet needs

Discounts self

NLP
EFT
KIDS

8. SET REALISTIC GOALS

Do your children set realistic goals? Do you? When we set goals that we can't possibly achieve we lose confidence. I expect you've heard of SMART goals.

S – goals need to be specific. Set a precise small chunk goal well defined and described as a 'towards' goal. It needs to be something you want rather than something you don't want. Hence 'weight loss' seldom works whereas making healthy choices does.

M – goals need to be measurable so you know when you've achieved them

A – goals need to be achievable,

R – they need to be realistic in that it is possible for you to achieve them

T – they need to have an end, a time when you will achieve it.

Encourage children to use this framework for their own goal setting.

You can set goals for even small events such as a conversation, thinking what you want to achieve perhaps in a discussion with a teenage daughter about what time she is to come back from a party. Go through the SMART routine to work out what exactly you want to achieve. This is called a desirable outcome. Having a desirable outcome for every situation and taking the time to assess what you want to achieve will be more confidence building than not having one because you deny yourself the opportunity to feel proud that you have achieved your goal.

9. <u>USE THEIR MAP NOT YOURS</u>

As parents we often judge our children by our own standards of confidence or our map of the world. Remember though that your child's map is different. It is much smaller and more intense. It is restricted to home and school for a long time and even after they go to secondary school, their world boundaries are still much smaller than yours. Whilst you will have lots of experience of talking to new people, being asked your opinion and having to discuss important issues, they will not. You can introduce them to your world and encourage them to make decisions and discuss issues and this will certainly help them gain confidence.

Another important point to make is that how you see them is not how they see themselves or how they think their friends and teachers see them. At home your child may demonstrate excellent confidence skills but these may be lacking at school. Similarly they may appear confident to their friends but not feel very confident in themselves.

Ask them how they feel. On a scale of 1-10 how confident do they feel at home, at school and in various other environments they are in? Give them skills for confidence building that will fit that environment.

To remove the emotion and get a different perception, a more balanced one, do the following: imagine you can float up above the situation and look down on it as if you were a CCTV camera. How does the situation look now?

10. REFRAME

As parents we are experts in placating our children and helping them to see the positive side of what may have been a disappointment. Again we are rescuing them (see Drama Triangle) but we can help them more by helping them to understand what went wrong, what skill they need and how not to let the same thing happen again.

Tell them that there is no failure only feedback. When they make a mistake they can reframe this as learning. When they come back from school downhearted by a low mark or a teacher's comment, friend's unkind teasing, ask them what they've learned from that. How will they put that learning into practice?

We need to demonstrate this ourselves when someone gives us negative feedback. By showing our children how we can take the learning from the situation they see how reframing works in practice.

AND FINALLY

My gift to you is the Circle of Excellence.

.

9 THE CIRCLE OF EXCELLENCE

Children can lack confidence at any age, from toddlers to teens. Show them the Circle of Excellence and they will be able to use it whenever they feel shy and overwhelmed. Here's how to do it.

1) Imagine a circle on the floor; you can lay one out using socks or tights at first. You both stand outside the circle to begin with.
2) Ask them to name a TV character or sports person who they think is brave and confident. Who would they like to be like at times when they feel shy? Talk about the character and what they like about it. Talk about a situation when it would be good to be that confident. What are tricky situations for them that you have observed? You can help them identify when they feel shy.
3) Now ask them to stand inside the circle as that character in the situation you have talked about. What would they feel like as that character? What would they do, what would they say and how would they feel. Ask them to pretend they are that character in the situation.
4) When they lose interest or go out of character ask them to step out of the circle.
5) Then remind them about the character or think about another character that they think is brave. You can use the words they use to describe the feeling they would like to have.
6) Step into the circle again as that character and imagine they are in that tricky situation as the character they have chosen. Again, ask them to step out when they get distracted.

7) Now remove the things you have used to make the circle and tell them that this is now an imaginary circle and repeat the exercise with the character they want to use.

8) When they can do this quite fluidly tell them that this is <u>their</u> imaginary circle and they can pick it up and put it down whenever they need to use it.

10 FURTHER READING AND FREEBIES

I hope you enjoyed the book.

Many readers liked the first version of it published in 2017.

*"This book is a **wonderful road map** to confidence for parents and children alike.*

The author begins by making the point that we tend to notice confidence by its obvious absence at times, which crucially means we focus on the lack of it, rather than on celebrating its emergence. She purposefully underlines the notion that what we focus on, we become. The book then reveals ***straightforward, practical ways*** *in which confidence can be nurtured and practised by how we look, sound, and project ourselves. Throughout, it is punctuated with questions to help the reader assess the measure of confidence within their own family, and I found this particularly helpful.*

Bartkowiak has written a short, sharp reference book which I'm sure many parents will refer to again and again. ***She has brought theory down from the clouds and planted it in normal, every-day settings - for which most of us will be very grateful."*** *Jackie*

*"Confidence for Kids' is a **well-structured guideline** to help kids getting more confident. It starts out with how we as humans notice confidence. In my opinion this book helps parents/caretakers getting aware of their own confidence and how to make it even better. One way of learning is to watch how other people do things.*

By showing confidence yourself, kids will know how to do it too. So both adults and children can benefit from this book."

*The author added questions and exercises for the parents to discover what they think confidence is and how they would like it to be for their child. This can be **a real eye-opener**, at least it was for me! Just like in her former books, Bartkowiak combines a lot of NLP techniques. She **explains them clearly in steps and makes them available to everybody**."*
Angelique

*"This is the second book I read by Judy. Her writing skill is wonderful - the book is **very readable**, clear with lots of examples and very practical. Also, after reading lots of parenting books I had the feeling there won't be anything new to me. But I was wrong." Tsvi US*

*"Very good and **inspiring**! I liked the clarity in the way the author writes and the simplicity of techniques and ideas." Pila US*

I've written lots of books. You can find them on my website judybartkowiak.com and of course on Amazon. If you've enjoyed this one, let me know you've reviewed it on Amazon to get one a free copy of Engaging NLP for Parents (free UK shipping only).

These next two are my most recent books.

JUDY BARTKOWIAK

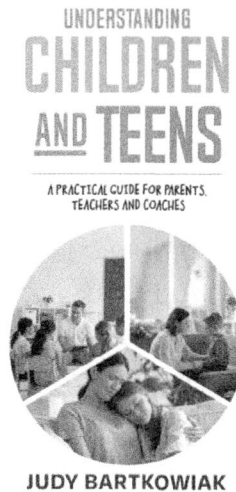

Here are some reviews from the original versions

*"Reading Empower Your Kids by Judy Bartkowiak is **like having someone take you by the hand and guide you gently through parenting.** Her book sets out to teach you how to coach your children through anxiety, sleep issues, relationships and friendships, and low self-esteem – while also learning about yourself and your reactions and emotions along the way".*

*"Judy's **clear and friendly and open language** helps guide you through established neuro linguistic programming (NLP) and emotional freedom tapping (EFT) techniques, clearly explaining the science behind these terms in an accessible manner. That the book is divided into two parts - the first exploring NLP and EFT and the second offering practical advice on supporting your child through a range of emotions they might encounter - means that you can access the information you need with ease.*

"Judy's book is a wonderful guide to the benefits of NLP and EFT techniques and how they can help you, your child and your family navigate the complexities of growing up in today's world." Katharine

"This is the best book I've ever read (Understanding children and teens) for helping coach and support my children to be their best, happiest selves. (And I've read a lot!) I found it **so useful I ended up writing copious notes which I keep to hand** for when I need them. Judy really knows what she's talking about in this area and I've taken so many of her strategies into my parenting." CR

"This was an extremely insightful and helpful book! (Understanding children and teens) Throughout this book **Judy's passion and expertise** clearly shine through. As a lifelong learner I consider myself to be very knowledgeable and this unfortunately means that I'm not always easily impressed. However, Judy's **writing style kept me enthralled** from beginning to end. She generously shares a wealth of NLP, EFT, art therapy and mindfulness strategies and exercises in a clear and informative way. **I have honestly learned far more from reading this book than I have from very expensive courses. This is a must read!**" Anon

"A well written, concise and easy to implement set of wellbeing tools. Even though I have experience working with young people this book has provided me with exercises that I have used straight away and to great effect. I see NLP, EFT and similar modalities as having a fundamental part to play in aiding the well-being of our future generations and …

this book deserves a place on any parent, carer or professionals shelf."

If you prefer bite size chunks – try my podcast 'Understanding children and teens' and check out all me freebies on my website judybartkowiak.com

Printed in Great Britain
by Amazon